MEALS IN A JAR

Tables of Contents

CHAPTER 1: ABOUT MEALS IN A JAR

Meals in jar recipes are super simple to prepare. The ingredients to be used are already measured and cut up so you simply take one or two steps to cook the food when you are ready to do so. Of which, in most cases, it's as simple as just adding water to the recipe at cooking time and the food is ready!

The jar comes in varied sizes and this can be prepared for the number of servings in your family. The meal in a quart-size jar can serve a family of five to six and makes approximately nine cups of cooked food. Canning jars are recommended as they are reusable. Mylar bags can also be used. A new lid is required when canning foods in a hot water bath, but the case is different when making meals in a jar. It's only your first time making meals in a jar that you will need to get a new lid and this can be reused another time. Mylar bags are perfect to be used for gift meals or meals for college students that will just dispose of the jar.

Meals in pint-sized jars are great for a couple or a single individual. The meal in a pint jar makes two to three servings, so you will not get tired of the food. You can divide the ingredients that will make a pint jar into two and use a half-pint jar if you desire one serving.

Meals in a jar are a better way to have a "grab and go" meal in any circumstance. You can take quart-size jars out of town when paying a family visit and you can as well take some of the recipes for camping. As said earlier, jar meals can be prepared easily and in most cases, all you need is to add water to cook them. In fact, these meals can be cooked by children, to know how easy they can be.

The meal in a jar shelf life is about five to fifteen years, depending on the ingredients used in a particular recipe. The shelf life of #10 cans after opening them is around six to twelve months. To extend #10 can ingredients' shelf life of after you have opened it, split the ingredients into mason jars and place oxygen absorber on top them. The oxygen in the jar will be absorbed by the oxygen absorber and the shelf life of the ingredients will be extended back to the actual life prior to the opening of the can. You're doing the same thing when you make a meal in a jar.

Note: do not keep egg products and meat in an open can, the ideal thing is to store them in a sealed bottle or refrigerate them.

To know the shelf life of a particular recipe in a jar; what you need to do is list out the ingredients you used in preparing the recipe with their equivalent shelf life. The ingredient with the lowest shelf life automatically determines the shelf life of your complete recipe.

Meals in a jar are the simplest way to prepare food for storage. No liquid ingredient is added to the jar and no pressure or water bath canning is required like the method we use to preserve foods that have liquid. You only need to measure the ingredients and place them onto the jar while ensuring the environment you are working in is dry enough; Place an oxygen absorber in the jar after putting all the recipe's ingredients and then place a brand new lid. This absorber of oxygen will remove the air out of the jar and vacuum pack it. You can also use a Food Saver with the jars but do not use Food Saver bags as the plastic is excessively porous

Dehydrated and Freeze-Dried Ingredients

Dehydrating can be described as a process whereby you slowly cook out the moisture within an ingredient without actually cooking it. You can do this using various methods such as dehydrator, sun drying, or air drying. Even as the process of freeze-drying requires large, costly pieces of equipment, dehydrating is a very easy process that you could even do at home. The dehydrated products take a longer amount of time to rehydrate due to the fact that they aren't cooked in the processing.

Freeze-drying on the other hand is a process by which cooked or fresh food is quickly frozen and then transferred into a vacuum chamber where it's being subjected to low-level heat. This heating process is being carried out in order to evaporate the ice in the food without returning it to its liquefied form. The freeze-drying process takes out up to ninety-seven percent of the moisture in the food and you can freeze dry virtually any ingredient or food item. Freeze drying doesn't change the size of the food when it's prepared. The time the food takes to rehydrate is shorter since it's cooked and all is required is to add moisture back into the product.

The similarities between the two methods are far more than the few differences. A freeze-dried food still maintains a larger amount of its freshness, aroma, shape, and color when food is finally prepared. Also, the food rehydrates quickly within a few minutes after boiling water is added. Rehydration speediness is one thing dehydrated foods might lack, but they make up for it in terms of space and storage abilities. Whilst both dehydrated and freeze-dried food's shelf life is similar, dehydrated foods are more storable and compact. The food shrinks in the process of dehydration, making its size smaller than the actual size before the food is dehydrated. To many peoples, this makes dehydrated foods easy to pack and use in situations that warrant food storage as well as on camping and hiking trips.

There is a difference in the cooking times for the two items. You can just place both ingredients in hot water for five to ten minutes to rehydrate. It is important that you understand the two products in order to know which one to use in a particular recipe. I will explain an oatmeal breakfast using fruit and oats a case study:

If you're making use of regular oats that have to be cooked for eight to ten minutes, dehydrated fruit is the ideal product to use since it also requires the same amount of time to rehydrate and cook. A freeze-dried fruit may slightly overcook if you make use of it in such a recipe.

If you're making use of quick oats that take just about five minutes to cook, freeze-dried fruit is the best product to use since it has been precooked and it takes the same amount of time for the fruit to be dehydrated. Dehydrated fruit won't go well with quick oats.

If you're making use of steel oats that need to be cooked for about twenty-five minutes, it is important that you use dehydrated fruit because freeze-dried fruit won't do well with long cooking times.

Using Your Own Dehydrated Fruits and Vegetables

Most dehydrated and freeze-dried products have a shelf life of 6 to 12 months after the can has been opened, and you can still store them in the can while making use of the ingredients. Nevertheless, do not leave egg products and meat in an open can. You need to refrigerate or put those kinds of products in a bottle or container and add an oxygen absorber for 1 to 2 days subsequent to the opening of the can. Once you place a dehydrated or freeze-dried ingredient in a jar with an oxygen absorber, it will hold the actual shelf life. You must prepare all meals in a jar in a dry environment.

If there is a need for you to purchase new canning jars, it is ideal to purchase wide mouth jars so that there will be sufficient space to place bags of ingredients. If a particular recipe doesn't require a bag of ingredients, you can use regular mouth jars.

Prepare ahead. Wash the needed equipment such as jars, cups, measuring spoons, and lids the previous day in the dishwasher and allow them to dry overnight. When making the meals in jars all items ought to be completely dry. It is also imperative to thoroughly wash your work surface and your hands.

Make use of a canning funnel when adding the ingredients to the jar. In most recipes, you will be instructed to first place larger ingredients in the jar and then follow by the smaller ingredients. Lightly tap or shake the jar in order to knock the smaller ingredients down onto the large ones. This is to help create space in the jar for enough ingredients to be fitted in.

If you are making use of your own dehydrated vegetables and fruits, you must ensure they are completely dry to achieve the desired result

In some recipes, you will be instructed to put items in a plastic bag in order to add them to the recipe separately. Don't opt for ziplock baggies when buying plastic bags. It is ideal to buy inexpensive sandwich size baggies that can be twist-tied or folded over the top of the sandwich. Make use of a gallon-size baggie when you need a larger bag. Make effort to take out as much air from the bag as possible prior to placing the twist-tie on the baggie. Leave approximately one inch-plastic above the twist tie and cut off the extra.

After packing all the ingredients into the jar, place an oxygen absorber on top of the ingredients or make use of a jar vacuum sealer attachment on the food saver. If the oxygen absorber seems not to fit well in the jar, push every corner down onto the jar to make it fit. After that, take out the dry ingredients from the jar's rim. Use a Lysol wipe or damp cloth to wipe off the glass before putting the lid on the jar. This is very important to help the lid seal the glass.

CHAPTER 2: BREAKFAST RECIPES IN A JAR

Almond-Cranberry Cereal Mix

Ingredients:

- 1 cup of quick-cooking barley

- 1 cup of regular rolled oats

- 1 cup of dried cranberries or raisins

- 1 cup of bulgur or cracked wheat

- ⅓ Cup of brown sugar

- ½ cup of toasted sliced almonds

- 1 tablespoon of ground cinnamon

- ¼ teaspoon of salt

Instructions:

- Combine all the ingredients in a quart jar.

- Put an oxygen absorber or use a vacuum sealer attachment. Place the lid and seal the jar.

- Attach label and date to the jar including the shelf life and procedure for cooking.

- Store the jar in a cool and dry place.

This recipe makes about 4 ⅔ cups of mix

Servings: 7 servings

- For each serving: Combine ⅓ cup of cereal mix and ¾ cup of water in a large microwave-safe cereal bowl.

- Cook the cereal (do not cover) on medium power for about 10 minutes or until it reaches the consistency that you desire. Stir only once while cooking. On the other hand, stir the cereal frequently if you are cooking on the stovetop.

- Stir before serving. If desired, serve with milk, which will increase the amount of protein in the cereal.

Nutrition fact per serving: calories, 300; fat, 5 grams; carbohydrate, 62 grams; cholesterol, 0 milligrams; sodium, 83 milligrams.

Delicious Hearty Pancake Mix

For a long time, pancakes have been a breakfast favorite. But this mouthwatering pancake mix stuffed with raisins and a little bit of citrus calls for more than a bit of whipped cream or butter as a topping.

Pancakes are not just for breakfast; make your DIY multi-grain pancake mix in a jar to have an easy and quick meal any time of the day!

Ingredients:

- 2 cups of all-purpose flour

- 1 cup of instant oats – ground into oat flour

- 1½ cup of whole wheat flour

- 1 cup of dried buttermilk powder

- ⅓ Cup of sugar

- 3 tablespoons of baking powder

- 1 tablespoon of baking soda

- 1 teaspoon of dried orange peel

- 1 cup of sliced almonds, toasted

- 1 cup of raisins

Instructions:

- Add all the ingredients into a quart jar in layers.

- Put an oxygen absorber or use a vacuum sealer attachment. Place the lid and seal the jar.

- Attach label and date to the jar including the shelf life and procedure for cooking.

- Store the jar in a cool and dry place.

To Make the Pancakes you will need:

- 1 Jar of pancake mix

- 1 ⅔ cups of water

- 1 egg

- 3 tablespoons of vegetable oil

- Add all the ingredients together, mix until well combined and the batter is a bit lumpy.

- Lightly grease a skillet or griddle with the vegetable oil and then cook until both sides are golden brown.

Flavorful Onion Roll Mix

Ingredients:

- 3 ⅓ cups of bread flour

- ¼ Cup of dried onions flakes

- 1 tbsp of powdered milk

- 2 tbsp of granulated sugar

- ½ tsp of dried parsley

- 1 ½ tsp of salt

- 1 envelope yeast

Instructions:

- Put the onion flake inside a small sandwich baggie and set it aside.

- Combine the bread flour, milk, sugar, parsley, and salt in a wide-mouth quart jar. Next, add the baggie of onions and yeast on top of the mix.

- Put an oxygen absorber or use a vacuum sealer attachment. Place the lid and seal the jar.

- Attach label and date to the jar including the shelf life and procedure for cooking.

- Store the jar in a cool and dry place.

To make onion roll:

- Preheat the oven to 375 degrees F.

- In a large bowl, combine the contents of jar, onion, yeast, I tbsp of vegetable oil, and stir in 1⅛ cup of lukewarm water. Mix until well moistened.

- Next, transfer the dough onto a lightly floured surface and knead for a moment; roll it into a dough cycle, cut and shape into 12 rolls. Then, let the rolls sit for about 30 minutes for them to rise. After that, brush the rolls top with butter and bake in the preheated oven for 20 minutes, until golden brown.

Easy Potato Sausage Meal

Ingredients:

- 1 cup of freeze-dried sausage crumbles

- 2 cups of dried hash brown potatoes

- ½ cup of cheese powder

- ⅓ Cup of sour cream powder

- 1 tsp of dried sliced onion

- ½ tsp of black pepper

- 1 tsp of salt

- 1 bay leaf

Instructions:

- In a wide mouth quart jar, layer all the ingredients in the listed order; shake the jar gently while placing each ingredient to give space for other items.

- Put an oxygen absorber or use a vacuum sealer attachment. Place the lid and seal the jar.

- Attach label and date to the jar including the shelf life and procedure for cooking.

To cook the meal:

- Preheat the oven to 375 degrees F.

- Next, in a large casserole pan, place the contents of the jar. Pour 5 cups of boiling water; cover the pan and let stand for ten minutes. Then, uncover and bake in the preheated oven for about 25 minutes. Enjoy!

Beefy Red Beans Chili Meal

Ingredients:

- 1 cup of Instant red beans

- ½ cup of tomato powder

- 1 cup of Freeze-dried cooked ground beef

- ½ cup of diced freeze-dried tomato dices

- ½ cup of mixed bell peppers

- ¼ cup of freeze-dried celery

- ¼ cup of freeze-dried chopped onions

- 1 tablespoon of chili seasoning mix

- 1 tablespoon of beef bouillon

Instructions:

- Add the red beans and tomato powder in a quart jar; shake the jar well so tomato powder goes down the jar.

- Next, combine the remaining ingredients in a mixing bowl and add to the jar.

- Put an oxygen absorber or use a vacuum sealer attachment. Place the lid and seal the jar.

- Attach label and date to the jar including the shelf life and procedure for cooking.

To make the meal:

- Place a saucepan over high-medium heat; pour 8 cups of water into the pan and bring to a boil. Reduce the heat to low, add the contents of the jar and simmer for about 30 minutes.

Ingredient for chili seasoning mix:

- ¼ cup of all-purpose flour

- 4 tsp of chili powder

- 1 tbsp of dried crushed garlic

- 1 tbsp of dried crushed onion

- 1 tbsp of minced red pepper

- 2 tsp of white sugar

- 2 tsp of ground cumin

- 2 tsp of dried parsley

- 2 tsp of salt

- 1 tsp of dried basil

- ¼ tsp of ground black pepper

Combine all the ingredients and store them in an airtight container.

Pancakes Mix with Chocolate Cherry

Yields: About 24 pancakes

Ingredients:

- 2 cups of all-purpose flour

- ⅓ Cup granulated sugar

- 4½ tsp of baking powder

- ½ tsp of baking soda

- ½ tsp of salt

- 1 cup of dried cherries

- ⅔ Cup of semi-sweet chocolate chips

Instructions:

- In a large bowl, combine the flour, sugar, baking soda, baking powder, and salt. Next, add the mixture to a quart wide mouth jar; add cherries and then top with chocolate chips.

- Put an oxygen absorber or use a vacuum sealer attachment. Place the lid and seal the jar.

- Attach label and date to the jar including the shelf life and procedure for cooking.

To make pancakes you will need:

- The contents of the jar

- ¼ cup (½ stick) butter, melted

- 2 eggs, lightly beaten

- 1½ to 2 cups of milk

Instructions:

- In a large bowl, mix the melted butter and eggs. Next, add the pancake mix; stir until well combined. Stir in the milk; continue stirring until dry ingredients are moistened.

- Place a large, greased non-stick skillet or griddle over medium heat. Once hot, add the batter (¼ cup per batch) and cook until the bottom side is golden brown. Turn the pancake with a spatula and cook the other side until golden brown.

Mouth-Watering Blueberry Scones Mix

Ingredients:

- 2 cups of all-purpose flour

- ¼ Cup of nonfat dry milk powder

- ⅓ Cup of vanilla sugar

- 1 tablespoon of dried lemon peel

- 2 tablespoons of baking powder

- ⅓ Cup of shortening

- ¼ tablespoon of salt

- 1 cup of dried blueberries

Instructions:

- Combine all the ingredients in a quart jar except the dried blueberries. Lightly shake the jar to create more space. Next, add the blueberries to top the jar

- Put an oxygen absorber or use a vacuum sealer attachment. Place the lid and seal the jar.

- Attach label and date to the jar including the shelf life and procedure for cooking.

- Store the jar in a cool and dry place

To make blueberry scones:

- Combine the blueberry scone mix, 1 egg, and ¼ cup of water in a medium bowl. Mix until well moistened.

- Next, transfer the dough onto a lightly floured surface and knead for a moment; roll out half inch and cut using cookie cutters.

- Heat oven to 375 degrees F and bake for about 15 to 20 minutes.

Pancake Mix with Almond

Yield: approximately 10 cups of pancake mix, enough for 4 batches of pancakes.

Ingredients:

- 1 cup of whole wheat flour

- 3 cup of all purpose flour

- 1 cup of finely ground almonds

- 4 cup of milk, nonfat, dry

- ½ cup of sugar

- 1 tablespoon salt

- ¾ cup of baking powder

Instructions:

- Mix all the ingredients in a large bowl until well combined.

- In a large bowl, stir all ingredients together until well blended. Store in a resealable plastic bag.

To make pancakes:

- Combine 2½ cups of pancake mix, 1 egg, 2 tbsp of vegetable oil and 1¼ cup of water in a medium bowl.

- Stir the mixture well until moistened.

- Grease a griddle and place over medium heat. For each pancake, pour approximately ¼ cup of the pancake mix onto the griddle and cook until the underside of the pancake is golden brown and the top is full of bubbles.

- Next, turn the pancake with a spatula and heat until the other side is also golden brown. Repeat the process until the batter is finished.

Yield: approximately twelve 5-inch pancakes

Potatoes Meal with Basic Sauce

Ingredients

- 3 cups dried Potatoes

- ¼ Cup of dried bell peppers

- 6 tablespoon of basic sauce mix

- ⅓ Cup of nonfat dry milk

- 3 tbsp of dry butter powder

- 2 tbsp of dried Onions

Instructions:

- Combine all the ingredients in a quart jar.

- Put an oxygen absorber or use vacuum sealer attachment. Place the lid and seal the jar.

- Attach label and date to the jar including the shelf life and procedure for cooking.

- Store the jar in a cool and dry place.

To make the potato meal:

- Preheat the oven to 400 degrees F. Take out the oxygen absorber; in a medium ungreased casserole pan, pour the potato mix, and add 2¾ cups of hot water. Stir thoroughly until well combined.

- Next, bake in the preheated oven for about 30 minutes or until soft.

Delicious Chicken Noodle Meal

Yield: 6 servings

Ingredients:

- 1 cup of freeze-dried chicken

- 2 cups of egg noodles

- ½ cup of freeze-dried vegetable mix

- 1 tablespoon of minced onions (dehydrated)

- ¼ cup of butter powder

- ⅓ dry milk

- 1 teaspoon of seasoning

- ⅓ cup of cheese powder

Instructions:

- Mix the chicken with egg noodles, vegetables, and onions in a quart jar.

- Shake the mix and add the remaining ingredients. Shake vigorously again to allow the ingredients to settle well in the jar.

- Put an oxygen absorber or use a vacuum sealer attachment. Place the lid and seal the jar.

- Attach label and date to the jar including the shelf life and procedure for cooking.

- Store the jar in a cool and dry place.

To cook the meal:

- Remove the oxygen absorber in the jar and pour the jar content into a sizable skillet pan. Then, add 3 cups of water and bring to a boil. Reduce the heat when it begins boiling and simmer for 15 minutes. Food is ready when the sauce is thickened.

CHAPTER 3: MAIN COURSE IN A JAR

Spanish Rice with Hamburger

Ingredients:

- 1½ cup of long grain rice

- 1½ cup of freeze-dried hamburger

- ½ cup of dried onion

- ½ cup of freeze-dried bell pepper trio

- 1½ teaspoon of all-purpose seasoning

- 1 teaspoon of dried minced garlic

- 1 tablespoon of dried minced ancho chilies

- ¼ cup of tomato powder

- ½ teaspoon of smoked paprika

- 1½ teaspoon of salt

- 1 bay leaf

Instructions:

- Combine all the ingredients in a quart jar.

- Put an oxygen absorber or use a vacuum sealer attachment. Place the lid and seal the jar.

- Attach label and date to the jar including the shelf life and procedure for cooking.

- Store the jar in a cool and dry place.

To make the Spanish rice:

- Place a large saucepan over high-medium heat; add 5 ½ cups of water and bring to a boil. Next, reduce the heat; add the contents of the jar to the water; cover the pan and simmer for about 30 minutes or until tender.

Sweet Corn Chicken Chili

Ingredients:

- ¾ cup of freeze-dried chopped chicken

- ½ cup of Instant brown rice

- ½ cup of Instant black beans

- ½ cup of freeze-dried sweet corn

- ¼ cup of freeze-dried green chilies

- ¼ cup of freeze-dried chopped onion

- ¼ cup of freeze-dried diced tomatoes

- 2 tablespoon of chicken bouillon

- 2 tablespoon of tomato powder

- 1 teaspoon of garlic powder

- 1 teaspoon of chili powder

- 1 tablespoon Ground Cumin

Instructions:

- Combine all the ingredients in a quart jar.

- Put an oxygen absorber or use a vacuum sealer attachment. Place the lid and seal the jar.

- Attach label and date to the jar including the shelf life and procedure for cooking.

- Store the jar in a cool and dry place.

To cook the chicken chili:

- Place a large saucepan over high-medium heat; add 8 cups of water and bring to a boil. Next, reduce the heat, add the jar contents and cook gently for about 20 minutes. Serve with cornbread or tortilla chips. Enjoy!

Beefy Vegetable Stew

Total time: 40 minutes

Yield: 6 servings

Ingredients:

- 1 spoon of powdered beef bouillon

- 1 cup of red beans

- 1 cup of mixed vegetables (freeze-dried)

- ¼ cup of flour

- 1 teaspoon of thyme

- 1 cup of ground beef (freeze-dried)

- 1 teaspoon of garlic

- ¼ cup of tomato powder

- ¼ cup of minced onions

- 1 cup of diced potatoes

Instructions:

- Prepare a quart jar (wide mouth) and mix the beans, beef, potatoes, onions, and vegetables in it by shaking. Allow the contents to settle.

- Add thyme, flour, tomato, beef, and garlic. Allow the contents to settle by shaking very well

- Put an oxygen absorber or use a vacuum sealer attachment. Place the lid and seal the jar.

- Attach label and date to the jar including the shelf life and procedure for cooking.

- Store the jar in a cool and dry place.

To cook the meal:

- Remove the oxygen absorber in the jar if you used it and pour the jar content into a pot. Then, add about 6 cups of water to the jar and heat until it boils. Then simmer for 30 minutes. Enjoy!

Cheese Sausage Lasagna

Ingredients:

- ½ cup of grated mozzarella cheese

- ½ cup of tomato sauce

- ½ cup of green peppers

- ¾ cup of sausage crumbles

- 2 ½ cups of rainbow farfalle pasta

Instructions:

- Combine all the ingredients in a quart jar.

- Put an oxygen absorber or use a vacuum sealer attachment. Place the lid and seal the jar.

- Attach label and date to the jar including the shelf life and procedure for cooking.

- Store the jar in a cool and dry place.

To prepare lasagna:

- Place a saucepan over high-medium heat; add the jar's contents and pour 3¼ cups of water. Allow it to boil; reduce the heat and simmer uncovered for 15 minutes while frequently stirring. When done, let sit for five minutes to thicken before serving. Enjoy!

Spicy Rice and Bean Casserole

Ingredients:

- 1 cup of long-grain rice

- 2 cups quick-cook beans

- 1 tablespoon of seasoning (all-purpose)

- ½ cup of bell pepper trio (freeze-dried)

- ½ cup of dried onion

- ½ teaspoon of cumin seed

- ½ teaspoon of crushed oregano leaves

- 1 teaspoon of crushed garlic

- 1 bay leaf

- ¼ cup powdered tomato

- ½ cup of cheese sauce powder

Instructions:

- Combine all the ingredients in a quart jar.

- Put an oxygen absorber or use a vacuum sealer attachment. Place the lid and seal the jar.

44

- Attach label and date to the jar including the shelf life and procedure for cooking.

- Store the jar in a cool and dry place.

To prepare the casserole:

- Preheat the oven to 350 degrees F.

- In a deep casserole pan, place jar contents, pour six cups of boiling water and cover the pan.

- Next, place the casserole in the oven and cook for 35 minutes. Enjoy!

Potato Cheese Sausage Casserole

Ingredients:

- 2 cups of dried brown potatoes

- 1 cup of cheese sauce powder

- ½ cup of sour cream powder

- 1½ teaspoon of dried minced garlic

- ⅓ Cup of dried onion

- 1 cup of ham or sausage (freeze-dried)

- ½ Teaspoon of cracked fresh pepper

- 2 cups (4 oz) of dried hash brown potatoes

- ⅛ Teaspoon of ground nutmeg

- 1 bay leaf

Instructions:

- Combine all the ingredients in a quart jar.

- Put an oxygen absorber or use a vacuum sealer attachment. Place the lid and seal the jar.

- Attach label and date to the jar including the shelf life and procedure for cooking.

- Store the jar in a cool and dry place.

To prepare the casserole:

- In a deep casserole pan, add the jar content, pour $5\frac{1}{2}$ of boiling water, and then cover for ten minutes. Next, bake in the microwave for 15 minutes or in the solar oven for 60 minutes.

- To serve, top with extra cheese, crushed crackers, or crushed cornflakes is desired. Enjoy!

Delicious Turkey Noodle Casserole

Ingredients:

- 2 cups of radiator noodles

- ½ cup of freeze-dried mixed vegetables

- ¼ cup of freeze-dried broccoli

- 1 cup freeze-dried turkey

- ½ cup of powdered cheese sauce

- ¼ cup of freeze-dried celery

- 1 tbsp of dried chopped onion

- 1 ½ tsp of all-purpose seasoning

Direction:

- Place the noodles in a quart jar.

- Next, combine all other ingredients in a sandwich baggie, place Put an oxygen absorber, or use a vacuum sealer attachment. Place the lid and seal the jar.

- Attach label and date to the jar including the shelf life and procedure for cooking.

48

- Store the jar in a cool and dry place.

To prepare the casserole:

- In a medium saucepan, place the contents of the baggie and 11/2 cups of water and bring to a boil. Simmer over low heat for five minutes. Next, cover the pan and turn off the heat.

- While the sauce is simmering, cook the pasta in a pot until tender and drain. Next, stir in the noodle onto the sauce. Serve onto a casserole dish; top with more cheese if you wish. Enjoy!

Rice Cheese and Broccoli Casserole

Ingredients:

- 2 cups of long-grain rice

- ¼ cup dried powdered butter

- 1 teaspoon of salt

In a separate bag on top of rice:

- 1 cup freeze-dried broccoli

- ¼ cup dried chopped onion

- ¼ cup of freeze-dried celery

- 1 teaspoon of all-purpose seasonings

- ½ cup of powdered cheese sauce

- ¼ cup of dried powdered butter

Instructions:

- Place the rice, ¼ cup powdered butter, and 1 tsp salt in a quart jar.

- Next, combine all other ingredients in a sandwich baggie, place it on top of rice inside the jar.

- Put an oxygen absorber or use a vacuum sealer attachment. Place the lid and seal the jar.

- Attach label and date to the jar including the shelf life and procedure for cooking.

- Store the jar in a cool and dry place.

To prepare the casserole:

- In a medium saucepan, place the contents of the baggie and 2 cups of water and bring to a boil. Simmer over low heat for five minutes. Next, cover the pan and turn off the heat and let it stand for five minutes.

- While the sauce is simmering, cook the rice with butter and salt in a pot over low heat until tender. Once the rice is done, serve onto a casserole dish and ladle broccoli cheese sauce over it. Enjoy!

Taco Rice with Ground Beef

Total time: 40 minutes

Yield: 4 servings

Ingredients:

- 1 bay leaf

- ½ cup of ground beef (freeze-dried)

- 1½ cup of rice

- 1½ teaspoon of salt

- ½ cup of bell peppers (diced and freeze-dried)

- ¼ cup of tomato powder

- ½ cup of minced onions (dehydrated)

- ½ teaspoon of smoked paprika

- 2 teaspoons of powdered beef bouillon

- Seasoning

- 1 teaspoon of minced garlic

Instructions:

- Combine all the ingredients in a quart wide-mouth the jar, shake the mix, and allow the contents to settle.

- Put an oxygen absorber or use a vacuum sealer attachment. Place the lid and seal the jar.

- Attach label and date to the jar including the shelf life and procedure for cooking.

- Store the jar in a cool and dry place.

To cook the meal:

- Remove the oxygen absorber in the jar and empty the jar into a sizable pot filled with boiling water of about 5 – 6 cups. Then cover the jar and simmer for 30 minutes until food softens. Enjoy!

Spicy Pasta and Cheese Meal

Ingredients:

- 2¼ cup of small pasta shells or elbow macaroni

- ½ cup of cheese blend powder

- ⅓ Cup of basic sauce mix

- 2 tbsp of dried butter powder

- ⅛ tsp of pepper

Instructions:

- Add the pasta or macaroni to a quart jar.

- Next, combine all other ingredients in a sandwich baggie, place on top of pasta inside the jar.

- Put an oxygen absorber or use a vacuum sealer attachment. Place the lid and seal the jar.

- Attach label and date to the jar including the shelf life and procedure for cooking.

- Store the jar in a cool and dry place.

To prepare the meal:

- Cook the pasta in a pot until tender and drain. Next, pour 1 ¼ cups of water into a saucepan and bring to a boil. Then, add the contents of the baggie to the water and simmer over low heat until thickened. Serve the sauce on top of the pasta. Enjoy!

Ingredients for basic sauce mix:

- ¾ cups of corn starch

- 2 cups of powder non-fat dry milk

- ¼ cups of chicken bouillon powder

- 2 tsp of Italian seasoning

- 2 tbsp of dry onion flakes

Combine all the ingredients and store them in an airtight container and label.

Delicious Hamburger Pasta Meal

Ingredients:

- 1 cup of freeze-dried hamburger

- ½ cup of freeze-dried tomatoes

- ½ cup of freeze-dried bell peppers

- ½ cup of Alphabet pasta

- ¼ cup of dried celery

- ¼ cup of dried corn

- ¼ cup of tomato power

- 4 tbsp of seasoning mix

Instructions

- Layer all the ingredients in a wide-mouth quart jar in the listed order.

- Put an oxygen absorber or use a vacuum sealer attachment. Place the lid and seal the jar.

- Attach label and date to the jar including the shelf life and procedure for cooking.

- Store the jar in a cool and dry place.

For the seasoning mix:

- 1 cup of dehydrated minced onion

- 3 tbsp of green pepper flakes

- 4 tsp of dehydrated minced garlic

- 2 tsp of chili powder

- 2 tsp of celery seeds

- 2 tsp of dry mustard

Combine all the ingredients and store them in an airtight container.

To cook the meal:

- Add 4 cups of water to a large pot. Bring to a boil and turn off the heat. Next, empty the contents of the jar into boiled water and let it stand for 10 to 15 minutes to rehydrate.

- Simmer over low heat for about 25 minutes until pasta is tender. Enjoy!

Broccoli and Chicken Stir-Fry Meal

Ingredients:

- 1 cup of freeze-dried chicken

- ⅓ Cup of chicken stir-fry sauce mix

- 1 cup of freeze-dried Broccoli

- ¼ cup of dried chopped carrots

- 2 tbsp of dried chopped onions

- ½ cup of freeze-dried green peppers

- 1 cup of instant rice

Instructions:

- Add all the ingredients (in layers) in a quart jar.

- Put an oxygen absorber or use a vacuum sealer attachment. Place the lid and seal the jar.

- Attach label and date to the jar including the shelf life and procedure for cooking.

- Store the jar in a cool and dry place.

To make the meal:

- Place a skillet over high-medium heat, pour 4 cups of water into it and bring to boil. Next, add the contents of the jar to the boiling water; stir thoroughly to combine, turn off the heat and let stand for ten minutes. Next, turn on the heat to low and simmer covered for about 25 minutes.

Ingredients for the seasoning mix:

- ¼ cup of chicken bouillon

- 3 tbsp of cornstarch

- 2 tbsp of dried minced onion

- 2 tsp of dried parsley

- 2 tbsp of sugar

- ¼ tsp of crushed dried red pepper flakes

- ½ tsp of ground ginger

Combine all the ingredients and store in an airtight container.

To make an additional sauce if desired

- Add 1 ¼ of cup water and ⅓ Cup of stir-fry seasoning mix to a small saucepan. Place the pan over low heat, while stirring frequently, simmer the mix until thickens. Next, stir the sauce into the chicken meal when done. Enjoy!

Cheese Chicken and Broccoli Alfredo

Ingredients:

- 1 cup of freeze-dried broccoli

- 1 cup of freeze-dried chicken

- ⅓ cup of basic sauce mix

- ¼ Romano dry cheese

- ¼ cup parmesan dry cheese

- 3 tbsp of dry sour cream powder

- ¼ tsp of pepper

- 1½ cups broken up fettuccine noodles

Instructions:

- Layer the broccoli, chicken, and basic sauce mix in a quart jar and shake it down, Next, add the sour cream powder, cheeses, and pepper and then shake it down to have space for noodles. Top the jar with the noodles.

- Put an oxygen absorber or use a vacuum sealer attachment. Place the lid and seal the jar.

- Attach label and date to the jar including the shelf life and procedure for cooking.

- Store the jar in a cool and dry place.

To make Alfredo:

- Pour four cups of water into a skillet; add the jar mix to water and stir thoroughly. Let stand for ten minutes. Next, Place the skillet over medium-high heat; bring the mixture to a boil, cover it, reduce heat to low and cook gently for about 25 minutes until noodles are soft.

Ingredients for Alfredo sauce mix:

- ⅓ cup basic sauce mix

- ¼ cup Romano dry cheese

- ¼ cup parmesan dry cheese

- 3 tbsp of dry sour cream powder

- ¼ tsp of pepper

Combine all the ingredients and store in an airtight container.

Creamy Chicken and Vegetables

Total time: 45 minutes

Yield: 4 servings

Ingredients:

- 1¾ cups of egg noodles

- ¼ cup of butter powder

- ⅓ cup of milk (powdered)

- ½ cup of vegetable mix (freeze-dried)

- ⅓ cup of cream powder

- ½ cup of peas

- 1 cup of chicken chunks (freeze-dried)

- 1 teaspoon of seasoning

- 2 tablespoons of minced onions

- ½ cup of cheese powder

Instructions:

- Combine all the ingredients inside the jar, shake the mix, and allow the contents to settle. (use a wide mouth and preferably quart jar)

- Put an oxygen absorber or use a vacuum sealer attachment. Place the lid and seal the jar.

- Attach label and date to the jar including the shelf life and procedure for cooking.

- Store the jar in a cool and dry place.

To cook the meal:

- Remove the oxygen absorber and pour the jar content in a casserole dish. Add 4 cups of hot water to the dish and leave for 10 minutes to rehydrate, cover the dish and at a temperature of 350°F for about 40 minutes.

Mouth-Watering Macaroni and Cheese

Yield: 4 servings

Ingredients:

- 2 cups of macaroni

- 1/3 cup of cheese powder

- 1½ spoon of corn starch

- 1 tablespoon of butter powder

Instructions:

- Make use of a jar with a wide mouth. Put the pasta in the jar and put the remaining ingredients in a sandwich bag.

- Seal the bag and put it on the pasta in the jar

- Put an oxygen absorber or use a vacuum sealer attachment. Place the lid and seal the jar.

- Attach label and date to the jar including the shelf life and procedure for cooking.

- Store the jar in a cool and dry place.

To cook the meal:

- Bring water to boil in a saucepan and cook the macaroni from the jar in the boiling water according to the instructions. Drain the water off and allow the pasta to sit in a bowl, add the ingredient-mix in the bag to the bowl of macaroni, add ¾ lukewarm cup of water and stir until it's ready to be served.

Spicy Pasta with Sausage and Mushrooms

If you do not have Italian seasoning in your pantry, use 1 tsp of dry basil, 1 tsp of dried oregano and ½ tsp of dried thyme.

Ingredients:

- ⅓ Cup of dried minced onion

- ⅔ Cup of tomato powder

- 1tablespoon of Italian Seasoning

- ⅓ Cup of freeze-dried mushrooms

- ⅔ Cup of freeze-dried Hamburger

- ⅓ Cup of freeze-dried sausage

- 1 cup of Ziti pasta (3 oz)

- ⅔ Cup of freeze-dried Mozzarella cheese

Instructions:

- Add all the ingredients (excluding mozzarella cheese) in a wide-mouth quart jar. Put cheese in a cheese sandwich baggie and place on top of the ingredients in the jar.

- Put an oxygen absorber or use a vacuum sealer attachment. Place the lid and seal the jar.

- Attach label and date to the jar including the shelf life and

- Store the jar in a cool and dry place.

To prepare the meal:

- In a large pot or skillet, place the contents of the jar (excluding cheese), add 4 ½ cups of water. Cover the pot, bring to a boil over high-medium heat, reduce heat and simmer for about 20 minutes until sauce is thick and pasta is tender.

- Next, put the mozzarella cheese in a small bowl and spray lightly with water. Let stand for five minutes. Then, remove the cover of the cooked mixture, place cheese on top and cover again. Let stand for five minutes for the cheese to melt. Serve when still hot.

- Top with cheese or sour cream if you feel like. Enjoy!

Rice and Chicken Casserole

Ingredients:

- 1 cup of long-grain white rice

- ¼ cup of freeze-dried cheese powder

- ¼ cup of veloute powder

- 1 teaspoon of salt

- ½ cup of butter powder

- 1 cup of diced-dried chicken

- 1 teaspoon of all-purpose seasoning

- 1 cup freeze-dried broccoli

- ¼ cup of dried chopped onion

- ½ cup of freeze- dried celery

Instructions:

- Layer all the ingredients in a quart wide-mouth jar in the listed order. Shake the jar gently while placing each ingredient to give space.

- Put an oxygen absorber or use a vacuum sealer attachment. Place the lid and seal the jar.

- Attach label and date to the jar including the shelf life and

- Store the jar in a cool and dry place.

To cook meal:

- Pour 7 cups of water into a large pot or skillet and bring to a boil over high-medium heat. Stir in the contents of the jar. Reduce heat to low, cover the skillet and simmer for about 20 minutes until rice and chicken are cooked through, stirring occasionally.

Beefy Taco with Cheese

Ingredients:

- 1/2 cup of powder cheese blend

- 4 tbsp of taco seasoning

- 1/4 cup of dried minced onions

- 2 tbsp of powder milk

- 1 cup of egg noodles

Instructions:

- Layer all the ingredients in a quart wide-mouth jar in the listed order. Shake the jar gently while placing each ingredient to give space.

- Put an oxygen absorber or use a vacuum sealer attachment. Place the lid and seal the jar.

- Attach label and date to the jar including the shelf life and

- Store the jar in a cool and dry place.

To cook the meal you will need one pound of browned and drained-off fat beef.

Instruction for cooking:

- Place the beef in a large saucepan, pour 3 cups of water into it and bring to a boil over high-medium heat. Next, reduce heat, add the contents of the jar and simmer for about 20 minutes until noodles are tender.

CHAPTER 4: DESSERTS IN A JAR

Delicious Brownies Mix

Total: 35 minutes

Servings: 6 to 8 servings

Ingredients:

- 1 cup of all-purpose flour

- ⅛ Tsp of baking soda

- ¼ tsp of baking powder

- A pinch salt

- 1 cup of brown sugar, packed

- 1 cup (approximately 8 oz) semisweet chocolate chips

- 1 cup chopped walnuts or pecans

Instructions:

- Layer the flour, baking soda, baking powder, and salt in a quart jar and then shake the jar a bit to level the layer.

- Next, divide the brown sugar, chocolate chips and walnut into two and add half of each to the jar. Repeat layer with the remaining half of the three ingredients.

- Put an oxygen absorber or use a vacuum sealer attachment. Place the lid and seal the jar.

- Attach label and date to the jar including the shelf life and procedure for cooking.

- Store the jar in a cool and dry place.

To make the brownie you will need:

- 1 stick butter or margarine (4oz), melted but lightly cool

- 1 tsp of vanilla

- 1 egg, lightly beaten

Instructions:

- Preheat the oven to 350 degrees F.

- Next, oil and flour an 8 inch square baking pan

- Combine the egg, vanilla and melted butter in a large bowl. Pour the contents of the jar and stir thoroughly with a wooden spoon. Continue stirring until the mixture is well combined and all dry ingredients are moistened.

- Next, transfer the batter onto your prepared baking pan and spread it to cover. Bake your brownies in the preheated oven for about 35 minutes. Enjoy!

Cookie Mix with Chocolate Chip

Ingredients:

- 1 cup of all-purpose flour

- ½ cup of brown sugar

- ¼ cup of white sugar

- ½ tsp of baking soda

- ½ tsp of salt

- ¾ cup of chocolate chips

Instructions:

- Combine all the ingredients in a quart sandwich baggie.

- Attach label and date to the bag including the shelf life and procedure for cooking.

- Store the jar in a cool and dry place.

To make chocolate chips cookies you will need:

- 1 large egg, lightly beaten

- 1 stick of softened butter

- ½ tsp of vanilla extract

Instructions for making cookies:

- Preheat the oven to 350 degrees F.

- Combine the egg, butter, and vanilla extract in a mixing bowl. Add the contents of the sandwich baggie and stir thoroughly with a wooden spoon. Continue stirring until the mixture is well combined and all dry ingredients are moistened.

- Next, cut the cookies to your desired size and transfer them to the baking sheet.

- Bake on the preheated oven for about 11 minutes. Enjoy!

Sweetened Cookie Mix

Ingredients:

- 1½ cups of all-purpose lour

- ¾ cup of white sugar

- ½ tsp of baking soda

- ½ tsp of baking powder

- ½ tsp of salt

Instructions:

- Combine all the ingredients in a quart sandwich baggie.

- Attach label and date to the bag including the shelf life and procedure for cooking.

- Store the jar in a cool and dry place.

To make chocolate chips cookies you will need:

- 1 large egg, lightly beaten

- 1 stick softened butter

- ½ tsp of vanilla extract

Instructions:

- Preheat the oven to 350 degrees F.

- Combine the egg, butter, and vanilla extract in a mixing bowl. Add the contents of the sandwich baggie and stir thoroughly with a wooden spoon. Continue stirring until the mixture is well combined and all dry ingredients are moistened.

- Next, cut cookies to your desired size and transfer them to the baking sheet.

- Bake on the preheated oven for about 11 minutes. Enjoy!

Cookie Mix with Oatmeal

Ingredients:

- 1 cup of all-purpose flour

- ½ cup of brown sugar

- ½ cup of white sugar

- 1½ of cup rolled oats

- ½ tsp of baking soda

- 1 tsp of cinnamon

- ½ tsp of salt

- ½ cup of raisins and/or nuts, optional

Instructions:

- Combine all the ingredients in a quart sandwich baggie.

- Attach label and date to the bag including the shelf life and procedure for cooking.

- Store the jar in a cool and dry place

To make the cookies you will need:

- 1 large egg, lightly beaten

- 1 stick softened butter

- ½ tsp of vanilla extract

Instruction for cooking:

- Preheat the oven to 350 degrees F.

- Combine the egg, butter, and vanilla extract in a mixing bowl. Add the contents of the sandwich baggie and stir thoroughly with a wooden spoon. Continue stirring until the the mixture is well combined and all dry ingredients are moistened. Place the batter inside a refrigerator for 30 minutes

- Next, cut cookies to your desired size and transfer them to the baking sheet.

- Bake on the preheated oven for about 11 minutes. Enjoy!

Gingered Bread Cookies Mix

Ingredients:

- 1 ¾ cup of flour

- ¾ cup of dark brown sugar

- ¾ tsp of baking soda

- ½ tsp of salt

- ½ tbsp of ground ginger

- 1½ tsp of ground cinnamon

- ¼ tsp of ground nutmeg

- ¼ tsp of ground cloves

Instructions:

- Combine all the ingredients in a quart sandwich baggie.

- Attach label and date to the bag including the shelf life and procedure for cooking.

- Store the jar in a cool and dry place

To make the cookies you will need:

- 1 large egg, lightly beaten

- ½ stick softened butter

- ⅛ Cup of molasses

Instructions for cooking:

- Preheat the oven to 350 degrees F.

- Combine the egg, butter, and vanilla extract in a mixing bowl. Add the contents of the sandwich baggie and stir thoroughly with a wooden spoon. Continue stirring until the mixture is well combined and all dry ingredients are moistened.

- Next, cut cookies to your desired size and transfer them to the baking sheet.

- Bake on the preheated oven for about 11 minutes. Enjoy!

CHAPTER 5: SOUP MIX IN A JAR

Creamy Mushroom and Wild Rice Soup

Ingredients:

- 2.75-oz package of Country Gravy Mix (no-fat or regular)

- 2 tsp of dehydrated crushed onion

- 1 tbsp of chicken bouillon granules

- 2 tsp of dehydrated celery flakes

- 1 tsp of dehydrated parsley flakes

- 1 cup of raw white rice

- ¼ cup of raw wild rice

- 2 tbsp of thickly chopped dehydrated mushrooms (oyster, chanterelle, or shiitake)

Instructions:

- Combine the gravy mix, onion, celery, parsley and chicken bouillon and place in a quart jar. Add the white rice, wild rice and top with mushrooms. Shake the jar gently while placing each ingredient to give space for other items.

- Put an oxygen absorber or use a vacuum sealer attachment. Place the lid and seal the jar.

- Attach label and date to the jar including the shelf life and procedure for cooking.

- Store the jar in a cool and dry place

To cook soup:

- In a Dutch oven or large saucepan, place the contents of the jar. Add 7 cups of water and bring to a boil over high-medium heat. Next, reduce heat to low and simmer covered for about 30 minutes or until mushrooms and rice cook through, while occasionally stirring.

- To serve, garnish with chopped parsley if desired. Enjoy!

Beefy Bean Soup with Lentil

Makes 1quart jar

Ingredients:

- ½ cup of elbow macaroni

- 1 cup of green split peas

- 1 cup of lentils (any kind)

- 1 cup of pearl barley

- ½ cup of dehydrated onion flakes

- 2 teaspoon of celery flakes

- 2 tablespoons of dehydrated parsley

- 1 teaspoon of ground pepper

Instructions:

- Place the macaroni in a sandwich baggie and set aside.

- Next, layer all the ingredients in a quart wide-mouth jar in the listed order. Shake the jar gently while placing each ingredient to give space for other items. Top the jar with the bag of macaroni.

- Put an oxygen absorber or use a vacuum sealer attachment. Place the lid and seal the jar.

- Attach label and date to the jar including the shelf life and procedure for cooking.

- Store the jar in a cool and dry place

To make soup you will need:

- 1 lb of ground beef

- 12 cups of beef stock

Instructions for cooking soup:

- Spray a Dutch oven or large pot with cooking spray; place over high-medium heat, add the ground beef and cook for 4 minutes or until the beef turns brown, while constantly stirring.

- Next, remove the bag of macaroni from the jar and add other contents to the pot. Pour 12 cups of beef stock, bring to a boil and simmer covered over low heat for about 20 minutes, while occasionally stirring.

- After that, add macaroni to the pot and simmer covered for additional 10 minutes or until macaroni is cooked through.

Chicken Tortilla chips Soup

- Yield: 3 quarts of soup

Ingredients:

- 1 cup of long-grain rice

- 2 cups of minced tortilla chips

For the seasonings:

- 2 tsp of lemon-flavored sugar

- 2 tbsp of chicken bouillon granules

- 1 tsp of dry cilantro leaves

- 1 tsp of lemon pepper

- ½ tsp of ground cumin

- ½ tsp of garlic powder

- ¼ cup of dehydrated minced onion

- ½ tsp of salt

Instructions:

- Combine all the seasoning ingredients in a sandwich baggie.

- Add I cup of rice into a wide-mouth quart jar, then place the sandwich bag containing seasoning ingredients. Next, top the jar with the tortilla chips.

- Put an oxygen absorber or use a vacuum sealer attachment. Place the lid and seal the jar.

- Attach label and date to the jar including the shelf life and procedure for cooking.

- Store the jar in a cool and dry place.

To cook the soup you will need:

- 1 10oz. of can cubed tomatoes and green chilies

- 1 5oz. of can chicken

Instructions for cooking:

- Take out the tortilla chips and the bag of seasoning from the jar and place them inside a bowl. Add the rice into a large pot; add 10 cups of water and every other ingredient (including the seasoning) except tortilla chips. Bring the mixture to a boil over medium-high heat; reduce heat to low and simmer covered for 20 minutes. Next, add the tortilla chips, cover again and cook gently for another 5 minutes.

Appetizing Taco Soup

Yield: 6 servings

Ingredients:

- 2 cups of black beans

- 1 cup taco (freeze-dried)

- ½ cup of diced onions (dehydrated)

- ⅓ cup of bell peppers (freeze-dried)

- 1 tablespoon of taco seasoning

- ¾ cup of corn (freeze-dried)

- ½ cup of tomato powder

Instructions:

- Prepare your quart jar; combine the beans, onions, taco, corn, and peppers in it. Shake the mix well.

- Add the tomato and top up with the seasoning. Vigorously shake the jar to allow the contents to settle well (ensure the smaller ingredients fill up the empty spaces created by the bigger ingredients in the jar).

- Put an oxygen absorber or use a vacuum sealer attachment. Place the lid and seal the jar.

- Attach label and date to the jar including the shelf life and procedure for cooking.

- Store the jar in a cool and dry place.

To cook the soup:

- Remove the oxygen absorber in the jar and pour the jar content into a sizable pot. Then add about 7 – 8 cups of water to the pot and heat until it boils. Reduce the heat when it begins boiling and simmer for 30 minutes until the vegetables soften.

Beans Soup with Chili

Ingredients:

- ¼ cup of dehydrated parsley

- 2 tbsp of taco seasoning

- 2 tbsp of granulated garlic

- 2 tbsp of dehydrated onion flakes

- 2 tbsp of paprika

- 2 tbsp of cumin

- 2 tbsp of chili powder

- 2 tbsp of white cornmeal

- 1 cup dehydrated kidney beans

- 1 cup of dehydrated pinto beans

- ¼ cup of small dehydrated white beans

- ¼ cup of small dehydrated black beans

Instructions:

- Layer all the ingredients in a quart jar in the listed order.

- Put an oxygen absorber or use a vacuum sealer attachment. Place the lid and seal the jar.

- Attach label and date to the jar including the shelf life and procedure for cooking.

- Store the jar in a cool and dry place

To make the soup:

- In a 12-quart pot, place the contents of the jar

- Next, add 1 medium chopped fresh onion, 4 15-ozs of can chopped tomatoes, ½ cup of cider vinegar, ½ cup of brown sugar, 1 big can of tomato paste, 2 pounds of browned ground meat and 49 oz of tomato juice

- Next, add water to cover the pot and bring to a boil over high-medium heat. Reduce heat to low and simmer for about 3 hours. Add pepper and salt to taste. Enjoy!

Nutritious Palouse Soup

Ingredients:

- 2 ½ cups of green split peas

- 2 ½ cups of lentils

- ½ cups of pearl barley

- 2 cups of brown rice or alphabet macaroni

- 1 cup of dehydrated onion flakes

- ½ cup of celery flakes

- ½ cup of parsley flakes

- Optional:

- 1½ tsp of white pepper

- 1½ tsp of thyme

Instructions:

- Combine all the ingredients and place them into a quart jar.

- Put an oxygen absorber or use a vacuum sealer attachment. Place the lid and seal the jar.

- Attach label and date to the jar including the shelf life and procedure for cooking.

- Store the jar in a cool and dry place.

To make Palouse soup:

- Stir the contents of the jar before using.

- In a large saucepan, add 4 cups of water of broth to a cup of soup mix. If desired, add a cup of cooked diced meat to the pan.

- Next, bring to a boil over medium-high heat. Reduce heat and simmer covered for about 50 minutes or until peas cooked through. Add salt to taste.

Turkey Noodle Vegetable Soup

Total: 15 minutes

Servings: 10 servings

Yield: 10 cups of soup

Ingredients:

- 1/4 cup of red lentils

- 2 tbsp of dehydrated chopped onion

- 1   1/2 tbsp of chicken bouillon granules

- 1/2 tsp of dehydrated dill weed

- 1/8 tsp of celery seed

- 1/8 tsp of garlic powder

- 1 bay leaf

- 1 cup of raw medium egg noodles

Instructions:

- Combine all the ingredients in a pint jar in the listed order.

- Put an oxygen absorber or use a vacuum sealer attachment. Place the lid and seal the jar.

- Attach label and date to the jar including the shelf life and procedure for cooking.

- Store the jar in a cool and dry place

To make soup:

- Place a large pot over medium-high heat, add 8 cups of water into the pot and bring to a boil. Next, add the contents of the jar to boiling water, reduce heat to low and simmer covered for 15 minutes.

- After that, remove bay leaf, add two cups of cubed turkey and one (10oz) pkg. of frozen mixed vegetables. Then, cook for an additional five minutes or until turkey and vegetables are tender and cooked through.

Mash Potato and Parsley Soup

Servings: 6 servings

Ingredients:

- 1¾ cups of instant mashed potatoes

- 2 tbsp of instant chicken bouillon

- 1½ cups of dry milk

- 2 tsp of dehydrated chopped onion

- 1 tsp of dehydrated parsley

- ¼ tsp of dehydrated thyme

- ¼ tsp of ground white pepper

- ⅛ Tsp of turmeric

- 1½ tsp of seasoning salt

Instructions:

- Combine all the ingredients in a quart jar.

- Put an oxygen absorber or use a vacuum sealer attachment. Place the lid and seal the jar.

- Attach label and date to the jar including the shelf life and procedure for cooking.

- Store the jar in a cool and dry place

To prepare soup:

- Pour ½ cup of contents of jar in a soup bowl, pour one cup boiling water, and stir frequently until very smooth. Enjoy!

Split Pea Soup with Lentil

Makes 10 cups of mix

Ingredients:

- 2 ½ cups of green split peas

- 2 ½ cups of pearl barley

- 2 ½ cups of lentils

- 2 cups of alphabet macaroni

- 1 cup of dried onion flakes

- ½ cup of parsley flakes

- ½ cup of celery flakes

- 1½ tsp of thyme

- 1½ tsp of white pepper

Instructions:

- Combine all the ingredients in a quart jar. Stir before using.

- Put an oxygen absorber or use a vacuum sealer attachment. Place the lid and seal the jar.

- Attach label and date to the jar including the shelf life and procedure for cooking.

- Store the jar in a cool and dry place.

To make soup:

- In a large saucepan over medium-high heat, pour 4 cups of water and one cup of the contents of the jar. Add one cup of cooked diced meat if you wish. Bring the mixture to a boil.

- Next, reduce heat and simmer covered for about 60 minutes or until peas are tender. Add salt to taste if you wish.

Instant Potato and Cheese Soup

Ingredients:

- 2 cups of instant coffee creamer

- ½ cup of ham TVP

- ½ cup of cheese blend

- 1 tbsp of parsley flakes

- 1 tbsp of chicken bouillon granules

- 1 tbsp of dehydrated minced onions

- ½ tsp of pepper

- 2 cup of instant potato flakes

Instructions:

- Layer all the ingredients in a quart jar in the listed order. Shake the jar gently before placing the next ingredient to give room. Top the jar with potato flakes.

- Put an oxygen absorber or use a vacuum sealer attachment. Place the lid and seal the jar.

- Attach label and date to the jar including the shelf life and procedure for cooking.

- Store the jar in a cool and dry place.

To make soup:

- Place the contents of the jar onto a serving bowl or soup tureen. Next, pour five cups of boiling water and stir. Let sit for about 5 minutes; stir thoroughly.

- Optional: add one cup of rehydrated cauliflower or broccoli to the soup. Enjoy!

Creamy Tomato Soup

Ingredients:

- 3 cups of dehydrated tomato slices

- ½ cup milk powder

- 1 tablespoon of sugar

- ½ teaspoon of salt

- ¼ teaspoon of ground cinnamon

- **Instructions**:

- Blend all the ingredients in a blender until smooth and place in a quart jar.

- Put an oxygen absorber or use a vacuum sealer attachment. Place the lid and seal the jar.

- Attach label and date to the jar including the shelf life and procedure for cooking.

- Store the jar in a cool and dry place

To prepare soup:

- Add 1 cup of contents of the jar to six cups of boiling water in a large saucepan. Bring to a boil over high-medium heat; reduce heat to low and simmer covered for ten minutes. Once done, add one tsp of butter or margarine.

Beefy Minestrone Soup

- 1 cup of orzo or tiny pasta

- ⅓ Cup freeze-dried green beans

- ⅓ Cup of instant freeze-dried black or red beans

- ⅔ Cup of freeze-dried ground beef

- ⅛ Cup of mixed green or red peppers

- ¼ cup of freeze-dried spinach

- 2 teaspoons of Italian seasoning

- 1 teaspoon of garlic powder

- ¼ cup of freeze-dried celery

- ¼ cup of freeze-dried sweet corn

- ⅛ Cup of freeze-dried sweet onion

Instructions:

- Combine all the ingredients in a quart jar.

- Put an oxygen absorber or use a vacuum sealer attachment. Place the lid and seal the jar.

- Attach label and date to the jar including the shelf life and procedure for cooking.

- Store the jar in a cool and dry place.

To cook soup:

- Add 4 cups of vegetable or chicken stock into a large saucepan, add a (16 ounces) can of diced tomatoes and a splash of olive oil. Bring to a simmer over low heat. Next, stir in the contents of the jar and simmer covered for 15 minutes, stirring frequently. Add more vegetable or chicken broth and 8 leaves of freshly cut basil if desired.

- Simmer for additional 10 minutes or until pasta is tender and desired thickness is reached. Enjoy!

CHAPTER 6: SALADS IN A JAR

Of course, you can prepare a salad (lunch) that will serve you for five working days in just about 40 minutes on a Sunday. You only need to prepare five jars and make space available in your refrigerator.

It's a pretty simple idea; begin by adding dressing into the jar and then layer different ingredients such as vegetables, greens, pasta, and cheese on top.

Refrigerate those jars until you are ready to eat them. Empty one jar in a bowl and the dressing will cover the entire salad. Enjoy!

Here are the steps to make a salad in a jar:

First layer: It is crucial to first add the dressing into the jar because if you add dressing last, it would make some ingredients that ought to stay dry get damp. That isn't ideal, especially when you are preparing jars for several days. Alternatively, you can prepare the dressing when you are ready to eat the salad.

Here are 3 appetizing dressings to inspire you:

Fortifying Sweet and Sour Dressing (enough for 2 jars):

- ½ of a lemon

- 5 tablespoons of olive oil

- 1 tablespoon of honey or maple syrup for vegan

- A pinch of salt

- A pinch of cumin

- A pinch of dried cayenne pepper or chili flakes

Peanut Butter Dressing (enough for 2 jars):

- 1 tablespoon of soy sauce

- 1 tablespoon of peanut butter

- 1 tablespoon of lemon or vinegar

- 1 tablespoon of honey or maple syrup for vegan

- 2 to 3 tablespoons of water

- A pinch of dried grated ginger

Honey Mustard Dressing (enough for 2 jars):

- 3 tablespoons of vinegar

- 4 tablespoons of olive oil

- 2 tablespoons of mustard

- 2 teaspoon of honey or maple syrup for vegan

- Pepper and salt to taste

Second layer: Add crispy ingredients such as tomatoes, peppers, celery, cucumbers, asparagus, red onions, carrots, etc. into the jar.

Third layer: Add the ingredients that do not need to be covered with a dressing, but not an issue if they get soggy. Examples of such are lentils, mushrooms, broccoli, corn peas, beans, zucchini, etc.

Fourth Layer: This level is for more delicate ingredients like hard-boiled egg and cheese (cheddar, Gouda, feta, and so on).

Fifth Layer: This is the level to add more substantial ingredients such as pasta, rice, or a more exotic item like couscous, or quinoa.

Sixth and the last layer: This is the final level and here you can add ingredients that are less palatable when they get soggy. Examples of such are nuts and greens spinach, lettuce, or arugula.

Next, seal the jar and refrigerate until ready to eat the salad.

There are endless variances for salads in a jar. So, heretics are allowed; you don't need to follow these six levels religiously! Consider it as a guide for newbies.

Some Salad Ingredients and How Long They Can Stay Fresh in the Refrigerator:

Here is a list of some common salads in jar ingredients. If you have more ingredients you are not sure about, it's recommended to check, Eat by Date, which is a very useful website when it comes to shelf life.

- Asparagus (cooked or fresh): lasts for five days

- Avocado: It is best to add avocado to the salad when ready to eat. Ensure to coat avocado with lime earlier, if you are to add it into the jar. With this, it will last for two days.

- Beans (cooked): last for five days

- Bean sprouts: last for three days

- Feta cheese: last for seven days

- Hard-boiled eggs: It is best to add them to the salad when ready to eat. An unpeeled boiled egg lasts for seven days while a peeled one lasts for two days in the fridge.

- Lettuce (chopped): lasts for four days

- Mozzarella cheese: last for seven days

- Mushrooms (fresh, chopped): last for five days

- Pasta (cooked): lasts for seven days

- Peas (cooked): last for five days

- Rice (cooked): lasts for four days

- Onion (sliced): lasts for seven days

- Scallions (chopped): lasts for seven days

- Spinach (fresh): lasts for five days

Some Dressings and How Long They Can Stay Fresh in the Refrigerator:

- Yogurt dressings: last for seven days

- Vinegar and oil-based dressings: last for five days

- Hummus: lasts for seven days

NOTE: It is important to always check if the foods are still in good condition. Endeavor to do the sniff test. The above numbers are just approximate.

How Long Can All the Ingredients in a Jar Stay Fresh in The Refrigerator?

Even with more tricky ingredients in the salad, it can stay fresh for up to five days in the fridge. But you will want to pay attention to the above ingredients. If you want your salad to stay fresh for five days, avoid adding ingredients that will not last that long.

The following salad jar recipes are a "grab n go" colorful and healthy lunch to take you through the workweek delightfully:

Basil Tomato Peach Salad

This basil tomato peach salad is a delightful way to enjoy fresh summer bounty.

Total Time 10 minutes

Servings: 2 servings

Ingredients:

- 2 tbsp of olive oil

- 1 tbsp of balsamic vinegar

- 1 peach ⅓ lb, chopped

- 1 tomato ⅓ lb, chopped

- 2 cups of chopped lettuce

- ½ cup of chopped basil leaves

Instructions:

- Combine olive and balsamic vinegar. Divide the dressing inside 2 pint jars. Next, divide the chopped peach and tomato on top of the dressing. Then, place the basil and lettuce to fill up the jars.

- Seal the jar and store it in the refrigerator until ready to eat. Shake the jar before serving.

Nutrition fact per serving: Calories: 183kcal | Fiber: 3g | Carbohydrates: 13g | Protein: 2g | Iron: 1mg| Fat: 14g | Vitamin C: 16mg | Saturated Fat: 2g | Sugar: 11g | Sodium: 13mg | Potassium: 407mg | Vitamin A: 1435IU | Calcium: 30mg

Spinach Pear and Quinoa Salad

This salad in a jar is loaded with protein-packed quinoa, pear, and spinach, this makes the perfect workweek lunch!

Total Time: 10 minutes

 Yield: 1 Quart jar

Ingredients:

For the salad you will need:

- 2 tablespoons of maple balsamic dressing

- ½ large ripe pear, chopped

- 2 tablespoons of pecans, chopped

- 2 tablespoons of thinly sliced red onion

- 2 tablespoons of dried cranberries or cherries

- 2 to 3 cups of baby spinach

- ½ cup of cooked quinoa

To make maple balsamic dressing you will need:

- 4 tablespoons of balsamic vinegar

- 3 tablespoons of extra-virgin olive oil

- 1½ tablespoons of pure maple syrup

- ¼ teaspoon of salt

- Freshly ground black pepper, to taste

Instructions:

- Combine all the ingredients for dressing in a mixing bowl. Pour two tablespoons of dressing into a quart jar (keep the remaining dressing for later use). Next, Layer the remaining ingredients into the jar in the listed order.

- Seal the jar and store it in the refrigerator until ready to eat. Shake the jar before serving. Enjoy!

Celery Zucchini Salad with Spinach Avocado Dressing

Makes: 2 quart jars

Total Time 10 minutes

Ingredients:

For Salad:

- ½ of cup shredded celery

- ½ cup of thinly sliced red bell pepper

- ½ of cup cherry tomatoes

- ½ cup of shelled edamame

- 1½ cups shredded zucchini

- ¼ cup of feta cheese, optional

For Dressing:

- Juice of 1 lemon

- ½ of ripe avocado

- ½ cup of freshly packed spinach

- 2 tbsp of extra Greek plain yogurt, 2%

- 2 tbsp of extra virgin olive oil

- ¼ tsp of pepper

- ½ tsp of salt

Instructions:

- Blend all the dressing ingredients until very smooth in a high powered blender,

- Next, divide the dressing into 2 quart jars.

- Layer all the salad ingredients into a jar in the listed order.

- Seal the jar and store it in the refrigerator until ready to eat. Shake the jar before serving. Enjoy!

Nutrition Facts per serving: Calories 298 Calories from Fat 206% Daily Value*|Fat 22.9g35% | Carbohydrates 20.7g7% | |Cholesterol 2mg1% |Sugar 9.2g10% |Sodium 638mg28% | Saturated Fat 3.8g24% |Fiber 8.6g36% |Protein 11.5g23

Chickpea Sprouted Spring Salad with Basil Vinaigrette

Ingredients:

For the salad:

- 1 cup of cooked chickpea, rinse well if using canned

- ½ cup of shredded carrots

- 1 cup of cherry tomatoes

- 1 cup of shelled edamame beans

- ½ cup of pine nuts, or other nuts you preferred

- 1 cup of fresh spring sprouts (onion, clover, mustard or alfalfa)

For the Basil Vinaigrette:

- 2½ tablespoons of red wine vinegar

- 5 tablespoons of olive oil

- 1 heap teaspoon of sweet Dijon mustard

- 4 to 6 fresh basil leaves, thinly sliced

- Coarse black pepper and sea salt to taste

Instructions:

- Add all the ingredients for dressing in a container with a lid and shake well

- Next, place the cooked chickpea in a mixing bowl; pour the basil vinaigrette over it and mix to be well combined.

- Divide the vinaigrette and chickpea mixture into 2 pint jars.

- Next, divide the remaining salad ingredients into the 2 jars in the listed order.

- Seal the jar and store it in the refrigerator until ready to eat. Shake the jar before serving. Enjoy!

Noodle Salad with Spicy Peanut Dressing

Makes: 4 pint jars

Yield: 4 Servings

Total Time: 25 minutes

Ingredients

For the Salad:

- 4 oz of soba noodles, cooked, rinsed and drained

- 1 red bell pepper, finely chopped

- 1 cup of shelled edamame, cooked

- 4 green onions, finely chopped

- 2 large carrots, peeled and shredded

- ½ cup of crunchy rice noodles

For the spicy peanut dressing:

- 2 tbsp of peanut butter

- 4 tsp of rice vinegar

- 4 tsp of soy sauce

- 4 tsp of sambal oelek

- ¼ cup of extra virgin olive oil

- 1 tbsp of black sesame seeds

Instructions:

- To prepare spicy peanut dressing: Combine the peanut butter, rice vinegar, soy sauce and sambal oelek in a small bowl. Stir well to combine. Next, slowly stir in the olive oil until blended. Then, stir in the black sesame seeds.

- Next, in your prepared 4 pint jars, divide the dressing equally the jars .Then, layer the salad ingredients into the 4 jars in the above listed order.

- Seal the jar and store in the refrigerator until ready to eat. Shake the jar before serving. Enjoy!

Nutrition fact per serving: Calories: 251 |saturated fat: 3g | unsaturated fat: 15 g Trans fat: 0 g | total fat: 20 g cholesterol: 0 mg | protein: 6 g |sodium: 455 mg | fiber: 3 g| carbohydrates: 15 g |sugar: 3 g

Black Bean Corn Salad with Greek Yogurt

This nutritious salad in a jar is filled with nourishing protein alongside a good serving of vegetables. Try this delicious recipe today and thank me later!

Total Time: 15 minutes

Servings: 5 servings

Ingredients:

- 2 cans of black beans drained and rinsed

- 1 1/4 of cup salsa

- 1 6 oz package of plain Greek yogurt

- 2 avocados peeled and chopped

- 1 red onion thinly sliced

- 1 quart of cherry tomatoes, cut into half

- 5 oz of block pepper jack cheese, cubed

- 1 12 oz packet of frozen corn, thawed

- 4 to 5 cups of thinly sliced romaine lettuce

- 1/4 cup or more of thinly sliced cilantro, optional

- 5 pint jars

Instructions:

- Add 1/4 cup of salsa into each jar. Next, divide the yogurt equally among the jars. You will have about 1 ½ yogurt in each jar. Then, layer the remaining ingredients equally among the 5 jars. Begin with tomato; follow with the sliced onions, then with the rinsed black beans, thawed corn, chopped avocado, cubed cheese and lastly lettuce and cilantro if desired.

- Seal the jar and store in the refrigerator until ready to eat. Shake the jar before serving. Enjoy!

Nutritional fact per serving: Calories: 449kcal Protein: 26g | Fiber: 21g | Carbohydrates: 68g | Fat: 23g

Summer Potato Salad

Ingredients:

- 1 ½ cups of diced freeze-dried potato

- ½ cup of freeze-dried diced ham

- ½ cup of freeze-dried celery

- ½ cup of freeze-dried chopped onions

Instructions:

- Layer all the ingredients in a wide-mouth quart jar in the listed order.

- Put an oxygen absorber or use a vacuum sealer attachment. Place the lid and seal the jar.

- Attach label and date to the jar including the shelf life and

- Store the jar in a cool and dry place.

To prepare salad you will need:

- ½ cup of mayonnaise

- 1½ tsp of Dijon mustard

- Pepper and iodized salt to taste

- Chopped green onions, optional

Instructions:

- Place the contents of the jar in a medium bowl and cover it with hot water. Set aside for about 10 minutes or until the ingredients rehydrated and tender. Then, drain.

- Next, transfer the drained ingredients into a large mixing bowl; add Dijon mustard and mayonnaise. Stir the mixture to combine well.   Then, season with pepper and salt to taste. Garnish with the sliced green onions if you feel like.

- Refrigerate for no less than one hour before serving.

.

Made in United States
Orlando, FL
22 September 2024

51806323R00082